# Strong in Faith & Business:
# 55 Bible verses for Christian Entrepreneurs

Sophie Frings

*Impressum / Imprint*

Bibliografische Information der Deutschen Nationalbibliothek:
Die Deutsche Nationalbibliothek verzeichnet diese Publikation in der Deutschen Nationalbibliografie; detaillierte bibliografische Daten sind im Internet über http://dnb.dnb.de abrufbar.

Die automatisierte Analyse des Werkes, um daraus Informationen insbesondere über Muster, Trends und Korrelationen gemäß §44b UrhG („Text und Data Mining") zu gewinnen, ist untersagt.

*Bibliographic information of the German National Library: The German National Library lists this publication in the German National Bibliography; detailed bibliographic data is available on the Internet at http://dnb.dnb.de.*

*The automated analysis of the work in order to obtain information, in particular about patterns, trends and correlations in accordance with §44b UrhG ("Text and Data Mining") is prohibited.*



Herstellung und Verlag (Production & Publishing):
BoD – Books on Demand, Norderstedt

ISBN: 978-3-7597-4968-0

Sophie Frings

**Strong in Faith & Business: 55 Bible verses for Christian Entrepreneurs**

**Table of Content**

# PREAMBLE

It was a completely normal Wednesday. I had just come home with my daughter after visiting my mother and was wondering what to have for dinner. Admittedly, I had used her nap on the train to continue working on another book project that had been lying dormant for a year. So I was kind of in the mood for books. Suddenly there was this thought that I should write a book of Bible verses specifically for entrepreneurs. There was no doubt, no room for much thought, just clarity. Two things I did as a result: 1. I went to the bookshelf and got my Bible. 2. I researched for inspiration.

The result was this book, for which I was simply a channel. I wanted to create it. Will anyone buy it? I have no idea! To be honest, I wasn't interested at all at that moment, because the focus was clearly on creating this book. No matter what happens after publication. In my mind's eye, I also saw how the verses were arranged. Each verse gets a page. A waste of space, perhaps.

Nevertheless, each quote should be given its space and the reader should not be distracted. The word should have an effect. It should have an effect on you, it should work through you. You should have an effect.

Love
*Sophie*

P.S.: When I translated this book from German into English, I thought that I should combine the verses with mit Line Art. This is how the Art in the end of the book was born. I am so glad you enjoy it, maybe frame it and let it be part of your daily life!

# BIBLE VERSES

For whatsoever a man sows,
that shall he also reap.

*Galatians 6:7*

Give, and it will be
given to you.

*Luke 6:38*

And the Lord said to Paul by a
vision in the night:

*"Do not be afraid, but speak and
do not be silent. For I am with
you, and no one shall attack you
to and harm you!"*

*Acts 18:9-10*

Trust in the Lord God
with all your heart, and
lean not on your own
understanding!

*Proverbs 3:5*

Ask, and it will be given to you;
seek, and you will find;
knock, and it will be opened to you!

*Matthew 7:7*

The Lord is my shepherd,
I shall not want.

*Psalm 23:1*

But seek first the kingdom of
God and his righteousness,
and all these things will be
added to you.

*Matthew 6:33*

O depth of the riches, both of the
wisdom and knowledge of God!
How unsearchable are his judgments
and unsearchable his ways!

*Romans 11:33*

May everything you
do be done in love!


*1 Corinthians 16:14*

The blessing of the Lord,
it makes rich, and he
adds no sorrow beside it.

*Proverbs 10:22*

Look at the birds of the air, that they
neither sow nor reap nor gather into
barns, and your heavenly Father
feeds them. Are you not much more
excellent than they?

*Matthew 6:26*

And who shall do you evil if
you are eager to do good?

*1 Peter 3:13*

Then he touched their
eyes and said:

*"May it be done to you
according to your faith!"*

*Matthew 9:29*

Fear not, for I am with you;
be not afraid, for I am your
God; I will strengthen you,
yes, I will help you, yes, I
will uphold you with the right
hand of my righteousness.

*Isaiah 41:10*

The heart of man plans
his way, but the Lord
directs his steps.

*Proverbs 16:9*

The Lord is my light and my salvation,
of whom shall I be afraid?

The Lord is the strength of my life,
of whom shall I be afraid?

*Psalm 27:1*

When you pass through the waters,
I am with you, and through the rivers,
they will not overflow you.

When you walk through fire, you will
not be scorched, and the flame will not
burn you.

*Isaiah 43:2*

I will instruct you and
teach you the path you
should go.

*Psalm 32:8*

Now that we have the
opportunity, let us do
good to all people!

*Galatians 6:10*

Watch, stand firm in the faith;
be strong!

*1 Corinthians 16:13*

There will be profit in every effort.

*Proverbs 14:23*

For with God nothing
will be impossible.

*Luke 1:37*

And be of good cheer,
for the joy of the Lord
is your strength.

*Nehemiah 8:10*

He gives strength to the
weary and abundance to
the weak.

*Isaiah 40:29*

*"For I know the thoughts that I think
toward you"* says the Lord.
*"Thoughts of peace and not of evil,
to give you a future and a hope."*

Jeremiah 29:11

Now these three remain:
*faith, hope and love;*
but the greatest of these is
LOVE.

*1 Corinthians 13:13*

*"And you will call on me, come and pray to me, and I will listen to you.*

*And you will seek me and find me; if you ask for me with all your heart. I will let myself be found by* you. " says the Lord.

*Jeremiah 29:12-14*

Come to me, all who labor and are
heavy laden! And I will give you rest.

*Matthew 11:28*

May the God of hope fill you with all joy and peace in believing, so that you may overflow with hope through the power of the Holy Spirit.

*Romans 15:13*

The grace of our Lord
Jesus Christ be with you!

*1 Thessalonians 5:28*

No temptation has seized you except
a human one; but God is faithful,
who will not allow you to be tempted
beyond what you are able, but with
the temptation he will also provide
the way out, so that you will be able
to bear it.

*1 Corinthians 10:13*

In hope rejoice;
in affliction endure;
in prayer faithful.

*Romans 12:12*

May the Lord bless you and keep you!

May the Lord make his face shine
upon you and be gracious to you!

May the Lord lift up his countenance
upon you and give you peace!

*Numbers 6:24-26*

For God has not given us a spirit of fearfulness, but of power and of love and of a sound mind.

*2 Timothy 1:7*

I can do everything through
Christ who strengthens me.

*Philippians 4:13*

Have I not commanded you?
Be strong and courageous!
Do not be dismayed and do
not be afraid!

For the Lord your God is
with you wherever you go.

*Joshua 1:9*

For it is the Lord your God
who goes with you;

he will not forsake you.

*Deuteronomy 31:6*

So that we may boldly say:

*"The Lord is my helper, and I will not fear. What will man do to me?"*

*Hebrews 13:6*

And the light shines in the
darkness, and the darkness
has not grasped it.

*John 1:5*

Rejoice always!

Pray without ceasing!

Give thanks in everything,
for this is the will of God
in Jesus Christ for you.

*1 Thessalonians 5:16-18*

A cheerful heart brings
good health, but a crushed
spirit dries up the bones.

*Proverbs 17:22*

This is the day the Lord has made;
let us rejoice and be glad in it!

*Psalm 118:24*

The Lord your God is in your
midst, a rescuing hero. He rejoices
over you with gladness, he is silent
in his love, he rejoices over you
with exultation.

*Zephaniah 3:17*

Wisdom reposes in
the heart of the wise.

*Proverbs 14:33*

You will make known to me
the path of life; fullness of joy
is in your presence, pleasures
at your right hand forever.

*Psalm 16:11*

Rejoice and be glad, for your
reward is great in heaven.

*Matthew 5:12*

For you formed my inwards;

you knitted me together in my
mother's womb.

I praise you that I am made in
an amazing, excellent way.

Wonderful are your works, and
my soul knows it well.

*Psalm 139:13-14*

Let us be glad and rejoice
and give him the honor.

*Revelation 19:7*

The Lord is close to those
who are brokenhearted, and
he saves those who are
crushed in spirit.

*Psalm 34:18*

But let us not grow weary in
well-doing, for in due season
we shall reap if we do not
grow weary.

*Galatians 6:9*

If you remain in me and my
words remain in you, you will
ask what you wish and it will
be done for you.

*John 15:7*

For the love of God has been
poured into our hearts through
the Holy Spirit, who has been
given to us.

*Romans 5:5*

Be merciful therefore, just as your
Father is merciful.

And do not judge, and you will not
be judged;
do not condemn, and you will not
be condemned.
Forgive, and you will be forgiven.

*Luke 6:36-37*

If he may stumble, he will not fall,
for the Lord upholds his hand.

*Psalm 37:24*

My help comes from the Lord God,
who made heaven and earth.

*Psalm 121:2*

# ART

When I translated this book from German into English, it occurred to me to combine my art with the quotations.

So on the next page you will find selected quotes with my own line art. Carefully tear out the page and frame it. Please keep in mind that this is only allowed for private use. Please contact me for commercial licence.

Have fun with it! You make me by the way extremely proud, if you send me a picture on how you used the Art!

**At least 5x7 inches (≈13x18 cm) necessary with passepartout or smaller**

The Lord is my shepherd,
I shall not want.

*Psalm 23:1*

May the Lord bless you and keep you!

May the Lord make his face shine upon you and be gracious to you!

May the Lord lift up his countenance upon you and give you peace!

*Numbers 6:24-26*

May the God of
hope fill you
with all joy and
peace in belie-
ving, so that you
may overflow
with hope
through the
power of the
Holy Spirit.

*Romans 15:13*

The grace of our Lord Jesus
Christ be with you!

*1 Thessalonians 5:28*

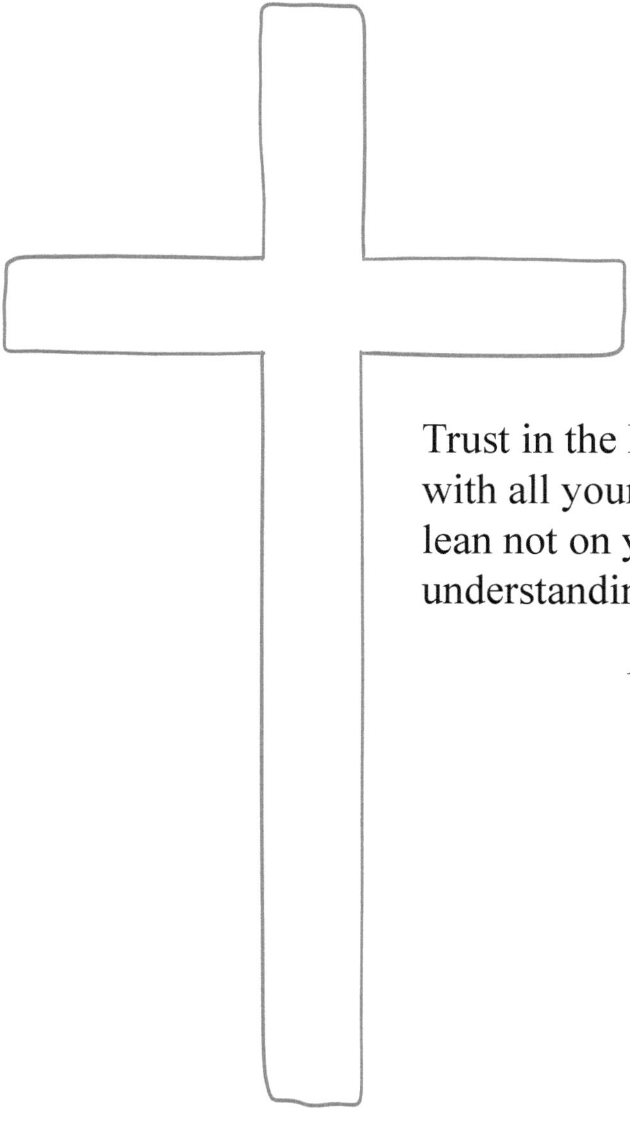

Trust in the Lord God
with all your heart, and
lean not on your own
understanding!

*Proverbs 3:5*

I am with you

*Acts 18:9-10*

For with God
nothing will be
impossible.

Luke 1:37

For whatsoever a man sows,
that shall he also reap.

*Galatians 6:7*

# GIVE

and it will be given
to you.

*Luke 6:38*

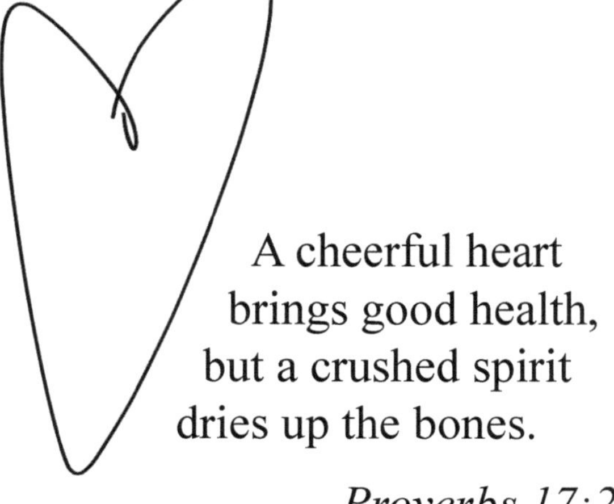

A cheerful heart
brings good health,
but a crushed spirit
dries up the bones.

Proverbs 17:22

This is the day the
Lord has made;
let us rejoice &
be glad in it!

*Psalm 118:24*

# ABOUT THE AUTHOR

SOPHIE FRINGS never did what everyone else did. In year 11, many went to the USA, Sophie chose Finland for the exchange year, which is why she still speaks fluent Finnish today. When everyone went to university after leaving school, she completed an apprenticeship as a baker in Düsseldorf. At night in a male-dominated environment, she learned one thing above all: quick-wittedness combined with self-confidence.

This is exactly what she needed a few years later when, after graduating as an industrial engineer, she advised managing directors in the skilled trades. A quarter-life crisis triggered by her father's cancer paved the way for coaching. She experienced first-hand how crises can be a great gift and what an enormous influence beliefs, patterns and (family) entanglements have on us. Since such blockages can easily be released, she turned her entire life upside down, quit her job and started her own business.

She now works online as a business and money coach and writes books on business management and modern spirituality. Her heart projects are her podcast and her online courses on financial education.

**Further information www.sophiefrings.de**